# Waterlogged

Asia Khatun

For her.

I thought I would be understood without words.

—Vincent van Gogh

# CONTENTS

Waterlogged

for oneself

# Her

I have noticed that all this time I have been writing a letter, one that never seems to end, to a figure who hides behind the fog. It's because I am useless when it comes to saying the things that really matter, the painful things covered up. The things I feel so deeply that seem to always elude my speech. Maybe that is why I surround myself with people who constantly fill the silence. The words I do not have the courage to utter, I hear them from the mouths of strangers. Sometimes I wish they would just ask me. What happened to you? I think they're too scared and I thank God they are. I don't have it in me; it's too bothersome. I want to forget the figure behind the fog. She disappeared long ago.

# Writing Back to You, Mother

Writing back to you, Mother
is like trying to trap a firefly.
The light is far too bright,
and my words cannot encompass it.
Will I tell you of my children?
The ones that have learnt to walk
and the ones that seem to always talk
in a language that I cannot understand.
Will I tell you of my husband?
The one that you chose
that works day and night
with dry hands, almost dryer than mine,
just to see me smile.

The distance between us only seems to stretch
further, Mother,
and my words are not enough to bridge the gap.
But when I write back to you, Mother,
the firefly seems to glow a little brighter
and that is a firefly that I cannot entrap.

# Stories

This language that I whisper,
I have borrowed it to tell you stories about the
people who stole mine.
Let me voice my convictions,
they are far more important to me than the optics
of blood-stained inheritors.
To speak is to weaponise freedom,
and to write is to caress its wings,
both of which I must do to survive.

# Old Friend

Old friend,
I have not seen you in many a month.
The seasons have come to pass,
and I, too, had thought
that the boughs of our acquaintance
had drifted afar with the cold winds
that wrought winter's sodden leaves.
But I have come to see
that our fair goodbye
was perhaps short-lived.

Oh, friend, why do you plague me so?
When a tear ought to dry with the mind's
acceptance,
why do you wish for the dams to overflow and run
evermore?
Is it not enough to pay for life's debt through
existence,
or must the windows shatter and the rain seep
through?
For it is not the rain I fear but drowning.

My dear friend, when the same sun casts out the
darkness in this world,
why do you insist I am to be shrouded by all that is
despairing,

or is it that you see this melancholy suits me so
well?

Friend,
I believe you know me better than many others,

or is it that you do not know me at all?

.

# The Sun

I have been carrying a child on my hip since the
moment I was born.
I know her deeply
and often I fight against my resentment;
it comes from a selfish ego, some hubris overlooking
my own mistakes—
of which I'm sure there were plenty.
I know you,
I know what the world has inflicted upon you
and for that I understand.
I wonder if you mourn what you could have had, too.
I was born in the shadow of what could have been
the sun.

I would take my existence and bury it in the depths of
the sea
if it were to provide you with a life truly lived,
but we make do.
We simply make do.

# Figments

Daughter of my bloodline,
there'll be no greater love that you will receive
than the two decades of what was never mine.
I shall betray all that I have ever known,
for an ounce of your happiness,
which I will measure in the creases of your eyes,
and if there is a moment you find
my overbearing self a fright
then I will be the first to let my blood run thick
and lay my head beneath your feet.

But it dawns on me that I will simply be a variation,
Daughter.
Perhaps no better, no worse.
I am afraid.
Love me. Love me as I love you.
You are a figment of my imagination and yet, I am
smitten and wholly captivated. I am dwindling,
Daughter, for your love.

## Life After

Sometimes I look
and I am foul with *why me*.
So, I look again
and I say *why her*
and then I wish it wasn't either of us.

# Departure

The evening dust blushes orange with the call of
my Beloved.
Every day I watch as life dances a little slower
around me,
when the clouds depart for the burning sun,
as the grey mist clears into a warmness I yearn to
touch.
The seconds of time weave themselves around the
muezzin's lips,
and like the birds that flock in the harshness of
winter:
the people, they run.

Even as the earth ties their feet to the ground,
their hearts chase the sound of Firdaus
and beg to see what lies beyond the orange dust
where my Beloved bides.

## Left Wondering

I wonder if I will forget all the things I wish to be
forgotten,
finally flee from these wretched memories.
Dementia runs in the family, you see,
but life is cruel
and I am almost certain
that I will only forget the things worth
remembering,
the few possessions that I have,
leaving me cold, dismembered and
wondering.

# Gold Reading Glasses

To love someone deeply
is to perhaps mourn what could've been.

A loneliness smothered with a familiar embrace,
an empty bowl of rice refilled,
a soft hand slipping yours into the pockets of a
woollen coat.
These are the moments I wish we could've had
together,
Nani.

I wish I could've oiled your hair and laid it pretty.
I wish I could've fetched you your gold reading
glasses and listened to you recite from the Quran.
I wish I could've cooked for you and the broth be
too salty.

Oh, I could've done so much, Nani,
but you are so far
and my home is here.

One day, when the cold returns,
this distance will cease to exist.
So, know that, from today
it is my heart that resides with you
whilst my soul cries and looks away.

# Munafiq

Feeling like I had failed my Lord,
I saw in the corner of my eye
a hypocrite standing before me.
She wore my face well.
Nose slightly crooked.
She looked at me, and she said:
"When the rays of dawn are fast approaching, why
do you delay?
When the peace of sujood awaits, why do you
delay? When your soul yearns for your Lord, why
do you delay?

أَلَا بِذِكْرِ ٱللَّهِ تَطْمَئِنُّ ٱلْقُلُوبُ

No doubt, by the remembrance of Allah are hearts
assured." 13:28

# Remember Me

Ever since I was a child, I have been leaving parts
of myself behind
in houses and cars and garden tables,
a ring, an earphone, a book,
clips and pens and purses.
I realised it's not the things I want returning.
Quietly, I have called these people back and
maybe it's not dignified to want someone to want
you back but
if I could make you remember me even after I have
forgotten my loss,
I would be richer somehow.
Then adulthood came and
there were only a few who returned.
Oh, remember me, remember me!
I am constantly aching with the death of my
memories.
They won't return, these things, my things,
clips and pens and purses,
this world will forget me like you.

# Lingering by the Water

Even the moon must wane for a moment in time,
some respite from splendour.
Mourning for these moments unlived is futile
and there seems to be so much,
cities and oceans worth of so much.
I keep lingering,
waiting for the tide to go out,
but it's waiting for me to go with it
and leave this place
for something else,
something better,
and every day I fight
to stay afloat
so that I do not drift ashore
to some place,
somewhere,
the moonlight cannot reach.

# Cool People

The people we create when we are young are so cool.

My uncle listened to Nas and he was an artist, school books and closet doors, characters and calligraphy unmatched by anyone else — who the hell was Monet. My uncle was an idol, not in the Godly sense but just in the way God had intended. When we are young, we don't know that people are allowed to be other things, blinded by our fallacies we are so desperate for them to be everything we're not. They are some semblance of our dreams in action and why would there be no sun in a dream? Well, over the years the sun declines its presence, not because he's bitter but because it's just life. It's how it's meant to be. The people we created were cool; they still are cool. They're just figuring some things out. Flaws, fights, whatever man. I don't care. You'll always be cool. I just wish now you would let the sun into your dreams once in a while.

# To Yours and Mine

In another world,
my dear Kafka,
I hope your tear-stained letter is delivered.
I hope all our letters are delivered,
yours to your father,
mine to my mother who sleeps in the next room.

We will not let the thing inside devour us.
I hope I am excused as you are
in this world where being lost
means you must be found.

waterlogged

I mourn what you may have known
if you had not mistaken my love
for your own insecurities.

## Rukhsar

I have you saved in my phone as
the bringer of hope.
You are an endless laughter that has exceeded
every moment of goodness
I have ever felt.
You are benevolence,
unconditional.
The only love that I hold true,
it is only love I see through you.

# Between the Ethers

The closest I have come to God
has been the furthest away from myself.
But I suppose feelings do not always dictate reality.

There is tomorrow
and then there is God's will.
I find myself tiptoeing between the two,
unable to draw breath
from the sheer volume of my failures.

# To Dream of Salsabeel

I dreamt that you were by the Fountain of Firdaus,
surrounded by those you had once loved.
All your worries had washed away with the gusl of
your jenazah
and you finally found peace.
She had been waiting for you all this time,
like a mother's womb, she embraced you
and your worldly strife fell beneath the seven
heavens.
Such hefty weights you had carried upon your soul.

How does it feel to be free?
The rivers that now flow beneath you
provide a coolness you have never felt.
The water wades through your sorrows
and your children are but mere reflections
underneath.
There is a warmth in your face, your smile.
There is light upon light.

I dreamt that you passed through meadows of
blossoming flora,
the soft echoes of hidden birds flickered through
the light and
humming a warm welcome, an out of sight hand
reached out to remove the bittersweet cloak that
tied you to this world.

waterlogged

A world that you so strangely understood
as being the most temporary dwelling.

Even years before you left, you had started every
sentence with
    *Remember, when I'm not here*
and the earth had deliberated with the wind
to only take you when the waters of Salsabeel
awaited.

# Selfish, as I am

In heaven, if I ever get there,
we're supposed to be thirty-three.
I wonder if He would grant me this one thing,
selfish, as I am.
To be a child once again,
to be the child before.
I wonder every day what she would have been,
what she could have been if.
My sweet, robbed child.
I run to you every day.
I realised I have been running all these years.
Maybe that is why I do not recognise the person
who stares back at me,
she is not supposed to be
and you are.
God, will you return me this child?
She is waiting for me, and I, her.

waterlogged

I have providence and these pages.
There is little else besides this ink
that desires to feel my presence.

for the world

# The Fraudulent Activist

I feel like a fraud
talking about the things I care about,
somewhere between a bystander and a zealot,
a martyr who will never rise to martyrdom.
I am sorry for my part in it.

# Creation

I held up a sign
to give the people water.
A man came
by the name of Creation,
parched and pitiful.
He had never tasted water before.

I held up a sign
to give the people water,
and Creation appeared once more.
He had used the hands I did not have
to dig at my well,
and I found him
no longer parched
yet, somehow, still pitiful.

# My Orphan

Have you wept?
I soon came to see the sickness through your eyes,
and then I saw the reflection of these children in
your tears.
How dust and sorrow filled their gasps,
extinguished their hopes with airstrike gas.
Bombed cold and never told that
souls are sold and bodies, too—
manmade green seldom speaks to blue.

And so,
it became an ocean deep with their starved bones,
and it is heaven high with their innocence alone.
Young tongues silences indefinitely
as frost and warfare burns, eternally.

*Mother, will you sing me to sleep as I sink?*
Morphing into something where humanity is void,
she asks in return with her dry, jaded eyes,

*Dead Orphan, how much is your oil?*

# My Beloved Will Wait

I had awaken dreaming of how the brown curls of
her hair would dance past my gaze,
how the corners of her eyes somehow shifted to
meet mine every so often,
and I could not help but paint the pale in her skin
with the pomegranate stains of my father's farm.
She felt like warm asal and hot qahwa on a
midwinter morning,
and after the stillness of fajr, I floated along with
the breeze until it delivered me to her.
I had found home in the softness of her lips,
watching them part as she read the sweet words of
Darwish and Abu Hayyan.

Another fajr came and I waited to be carried to her.
Instead, a broken accent pushed himself through
my door and said "ta'al ma'ana."
Baba was gone with the shuhada of Nablus
so, I left Mama staring at the barrel of a gun
as they dragged me from the clutches of the very
soil that had given me life.

For the next four hundred and thirty-one days, I
woke only dreaming of her in my arms
as I lay inside a concrete box, purple and naked,
with whispers of martyrdom
interrupted by the kicks of blonde foreigners

who had traded in their humanity for a piece of my
home.

Then one dawn, after my screams had fallen dry
and quiet, I found myself on the road following the
memory of her.
I returned to the soil that resembled the man I had
left behind.

He did not greet me well.
Rather, he had buried every inch of what I once
knew in dirt and rubble, and the neighbours told
me Mama's jenazah had passed with the wet leaves
of Autumn.

I asked of Leyla, they told me she had married and
left Nablus.

# 1971

The hidden women,
saree-clad,
behind husbands, behind sons,
under beds and in armoires,
with babies on hips and babies within,
running to the trees, running to the off-beat streets,
hunting for mercy
whilst they hunt for something else.

Bellies open and blood splayed,
boot prints over their forebrains,
a bottle of something for your troubles,
to kill what is inside, to kill what you cannot hide.
A generation of ghosts
waiting for no one, not even those who sit in
denial.
Your bastards lie in mass graves,
even the ones that escaped are trapped there trying
to flee in vain.

By the neck, on the day of reckoning,
what is hidden will cease to be
and the hunt for mercy will begin once again.

# Those Amongst Us Void of Compassion

*My* parents came here *legally*, she says.
*They* came on a plane, she says.

A shipwreck for your plane, then.

A waterlogged toy boat,
my child in the water for your child in the air,
one to drown and one to breathe.
I hold her up to the sky,
hoping God sees her
and sends me a guiding light,
the same one the child in the air has,
and takes her from me
as my legs seize,
and my face sinks.
My waterlogged child to the sky.

# Signifiers

Mangoes and marigolds.
Surely there is so much more to us
than the things we left behind.

# Liberté

Born in a land that had hunted my mother-tongue,
the place I called home had fed me half full,
but home had offered me liberty, you see,
away from my mother-tongue's encroaching
mouth.
*She* wanted to devour me,
whilst home placed bread upon my father's table.

Home told me my mother was wretched, and my
father barbaric.
He pointed at my head and laughed,
he said to me,
   Is this the liberty I have afforded you?

I felt him undress me with his imperial gaze as he
had done my mother and her mother before her,
those buried back and festering but I lived to be
studied amongst the stolen.
He pointed once more at my head and he said,
   Take it off. Let me see my liberty.
Did he mean *my* liberty?

   Don't you see your mother-tongue has
   almost eaten you whole.
   The plates on your table lie empty and
   your father stands starved.

And then I watched carefully as the pit of fire in
my mother-tongue's belly
fled up the walls of my home.
He began to melt, to drip naked onto the table—
a table sprawled with lies only circled by the beastly
flies that had hid all those centuries worth of
unlawful cries.

The fire stared back at me, and I saw that my
mother-tongue had been cradling me all this time.
She had been lulling me to sleep as home
attempted to thrust his liberty upon me.
The mirrors began to liquify
and I saw what was mine was still upon my head,
draped like my mother's and her mother's before
her and,
raging amber, my liberty wrapped itself around
home like a noose.
As he gasped for air, my mother tongue whispered
something in his ear,

It is Justice, I seek.

The noose slipped loose and home lay naked like
stone for all of eternity.
For that was what he desired,
and who was I to offer him my liberty?

# Palanquin

As the doves were set free in my father's palace,
I left on a palanquin,
wondering if he would still search for his sword-
less daughter.

Don't worry, Father.
It is in the indigo skies that I ran in silence,
and in the moonlit waters that I withstood
life's longing.

They had said that the flowers bloomed pale from
my lips.
They had said that you did not search for me.

# Glory

Slave money
tiles the streets I walk,
plaques for the tyrants and enablers
that want us to rejoice,
the warmongers and white supremacists,
glory, glory,
not to the bodies piled high in foreign fields—
the black and brown ones, too.
No, they will stay beneath the bank teller's note
whilst we sit in memoriam those decrepit printed
faces
that haunt the tiles of the street
my children will walk.

# Revolution

Revolution beckons blood.
I'm sorry to say it knows no other currency, but
where both the innocent and guilty are bled
and the spoils of war are bartered for between the
legs of weapons dealers and our clandestine peace
corps.

Revolution beckons blood.
I'm sorry to say it knows no other master
than the rejection of bygone pleas turned sour,
turned sour and begotten by the crack of the ever-
colonial whip that returns with it
the broken spines of supposedly God's young
image.

The sky grows darker;
the earth burns brighter;
the sea turns fiercer.
There is much else left to fight for
so that the dogs of yesterday howl no more.

# ABOUT THE AUTHOR

Asia Khatun is a poet and founder of online literary platform Thawra. She received a BA (Hons) in English and Creative Writing and has since worked on making the literary scene more inclusive and accessible. With a Bengali Muslim background, she discusses these facets of diasporic culture and spirituality within her debut pamphlet.

Printed in Great Britain
by Amazon

15827716R00038